Journey of Discovery

Journey of Discovery

Paula Denise Johnson

iUniverse, Inc.
New York Lincoln Shanghai

Journey of Discovery

iUniverse, Inc.

For information address:
iUniverse, Inc.
2021 Pine Lake Road, Suite 100
Lincoln, NE 68512
www.iuniverse.com

ISBN: 0-595-31402-3

Printed in the United States of America

"When I discover who I am then I will be free"

Ralph Ellison

Contents

ACKNOWLEDGEMENTS

First and foremost, I must give thanks to my Lord and Savior Jesus Christ. If it wasn't for him I wouldn't be here and doing what I'm doing. In the first book, I made the mistake of naming individuals, and some people felt left out so this time, I'm going to keep it short and sweet. I must thank my wonderful parents, brothers and sisters, nieces and nephew, cousins, uncles, aunts and all my dear friends. I love you all soooooooooooo much!!!

Journey Of Discovery

Join me in this journey of discovery.
I have discovered me and I am completely free.
I know what I want.
I know who I am and I am not afraid to show it.
This is my moment in time.
I am emerging.
I have risen above my circumstances and this is my time.
I am delighted to have finally discovered Paula.
For years I didn't know who she really was.
No more compromising.
Today, I am free and no one can take that from me.
No more hoping and wishing,
Only Accomplishing.
I am very proud of my discovery.
I am a lovely flower that continues to bloom and bloom.

Hidden Realm

Your girl is back to reveal the unknown.
I will speak of things hidden.
I choose to write things hidden.
Writing has allowed me to communicate to the world.
Opening the window to my soul.
Brace yourself because you are about to enter my hidden
  realm.
The hidden world of Paula Denise Johnson is about to
  become known.
Please know that this is my world and you are only
  visiting.
You don't know me, but you're about to.
Welcome to my world.

At the ages of 11 and 12 I contemplated suicide.
It started out with the sexual abuse setting the stage for
  low self-esteem.
No one knew the hurt and pain I kept hidden deep inside.
Because a phony smile had been painted on my face to
  hide the frown that my body wore.
Pains of the past haunted my young soul.
It's not always easy to see exactly what someone needs.
But know that words do sow seeds.
Seeds into that person's life that could either work or hurt.
Callous words and acts sown by the abusers caused me to
  believe that I wasn't worth living.
For years I blamed myself before I realized that "it" wasn't
  my fault.
You were sick and what happened to me had nothing to
  do with me at all.
I was only a child, for crying out loud!

When something bad happens to you as a child, it can take a toll on your self-esteem.

Who would have imagined that it would have taken this many years to realize that I am beautiful.

The pain was not big enough to keep me down.

So small and yet so powerful, who would have thought such a small and delicate being was keeping this deep, dark secret.

I now realize, why I wasn't the result of a miscarriage.

Or why I wasn't the victim of my own suicidal tendencies.

I am here for a reason.

All of heaven is rejoicing.

Not because an angel has fallen from the sky,

But because a mortal being has discovered who she is.

You Didn't Rescue Me, But I Survived

I needed you to rescue me,
But you didn't rescue me.
Why didn't you see the signs?
You know, when I began wetting the bed.
Or when I started acting up in school.
Didn't you love me?
The signs were there, begging you to rescue me.
Do you want to know how I dealt with this pain?
Never underestimate the pains of the past.
Well, I contemplated suicide while others turned to drugs
    and alcohol
Oh, you thought "it" only happened to me.
No, he molested "baby boy" and "baby girl" too.
It's not always easy to see exactly what someone needs.
But the signs were there.
Why didn't you rescue me when he was touching me?
I don't know who I am.
I am so confused.
Confused about my own sexuality.
Questions regarding my virginity still plague me because
    "it" happened to me when I was only 7.
And continued for almost 5 painful years.
I tried to block out most of "it",
But I still remember him touching me in ways he
    shouldn't have.
Doing things that just weren't right.
All the obvious signs were there, but still you didn't rescue
    me.
Even though he told me not to tell, the tell tale signs were
    there as I began to tell tales.

I remember the basement because that's where "it" always
   happened.

I hated to go down there.

I remember the many nights I cried myself to sleep.

Through the night my pillow was stained with tears.

And the next morning I'd awaken to my urine stained
   mattress.

In class, I wondered how many other boys and girls were
   keeping the same secret.

This is the cause of my bulimia, anorexia, and drug use.

Also, I believe this is the cause of my homosexuality,
   promiscuity, bisexuality, or whatever you want to call
   it.

I don't know how to love a man, let alone, let a man love
   me.

I don't remember exactly what made it stop, but I do
   remember that you didn't rescue me.

I was silent for too long, but I won't be silent anymore.

I will utter things hidden.

Not only will I tell the world what the abusers did to me,

But I will tell them how I survived.

The Healing Begins

I know I shouldn't feel this way, but I hate you.
I hate you for what you did to me.
I hate what you've done to this family.
Including your children, leaving them without a father.
The other victims have forgiven you, but I won't.
Although, at some point, I thought I did, but I can't.
I will never forget, let alone forgive.
There is no love for you in my heart.
I'm not proud of this feeling, either.
In fact, I hate that I hate you.
Yes, I hate that I hate you.
No, it doesn't make sense,
But if you were to die today, I can honestly say I will not
    find a tear to shed for you.
This anger has been held in for so many years.
There is so much hatred in me for you.
I just want to be free.
I need to be free.
Lord, please free my mind!
Please let the healing process begin.

A Writer And A Fighter

If it doesn't come from God,
It doesn't come at all.
I give you what he gives me.
If you don't like it please see him.
If you do like it please see him.
It's a gift and the words just come.
Usually it's in the middle of the night.
No one can teach me how to write.
Like I said before, it comes from my Creator.
I can't force it,
No matter how many times I try to sit down and write.
Sometimes it's a struggle,
Because I am a writer and a fighter.
My left hand is so powerful because it's the hand I write
    with.
I am very powerful when I write, annihilating haters with
    a lethal lyrical phrase.
Not letting anyone steal my voice, I fight with powerful
    words.
I must never forget where my strength originated.
It's more than just words.
The thoughts come so quickly.
Most of the time I can't even control the flow.
So I pick up my pen and just let go.
Through writing I have found freedom.
Freedom to speak whatever I like,
And share my talent by giving to you what has been given
    to me.
For each lyrical phrase has been given to me.
If he doesn't give it, then I don't bring it.

How and when, I do not choose.
But it's use I do.
I can keep it bottled in and die,
Or express this wonderful gift within and live.
I choose to live.
Therefore, I write.

Woman Of Fire

Some are fooled by her small stature.
And move in to take advantage of her delicacy.
But one would be insane to mess with her,
Or to even speak ill of her greatness.
I beg you not to mess with her.
There is so much strength inside this woman that remains to be seen.
With that powerful left hand, she is a great writer and fighter.
She will annihilate anyone who tries to harm her with many lethal lyrical phrases.
Very dedicated to writing,
While others are sleeping, she is awake and writing.
People are often amazed at this small but forceful woman's ability to move mountains.
She is even amazed at her own strengths.
When I look at her I see beauty no one knew before.
Those beautiful brown eyes captivates all who dare to gaze in them.
Her inner strength has made her more beautiful than ever before.
Egotistical?
Not at all.
Only the uninformed would mistake her confidence for arrogance.
Paula Denise Johnson is a Precious, Delicate Jewel.

Beauty No One Knew

When I look at you,

I see beauty no one knew.

Your inner strength has made you more beautiful than
ever before.

You were not always this way.

And it took some time,

But you now realize that beauty is your name.

It's been a long time coming,

But here you are.

A magnificent being, captivating all who dare to look into
your eyes.

God created your beauty and no one can take away your
beauty, not even time.

Some only possess outer beauty, but you possess both.

It's not just your outer beauty,

Or somewhat curvaceous body that makes you beautiful.

But it's your award winning personality that makes you
this way.

You may have all the pulchritude in the world, but if you
don't possess it within,

It's meaningless.

You are truly a sight to behold and adored by many.

Away With Religion

There are so many churches in America.

We are a very religious country, but also very racists, hateful and wicked.

Passions of Christ's crucifixion has rendered insurmountable controversy, but I don't know of any crucifixion that would be a pretty sight.

Why all the uproar?

We kill, we hate, and yet we love God, so we say.

Prayer has been taken out of our schools, but our money is engraved with the words "IN GOD WE TRUST".

This validates my belief that it is not religion nor mere words that save us, but a true relationship with the creator.

Away with religion!

To have a true relationship with God, this is my desire.

Lord, what is it that you would have me to do?

I am here unworthy to stand before you,

But I come to you with my head unbowed.

I am brought to my knees in adoration of you.

I've never known one so worthy of ALL praise.

I have searched the dictionary and not to my surprise, there are NO WORDS to describe your greatness.

Amazed at every single thing you do for me, I can't even imagine what you would do if I was worthy.

It's sometimes strange how we are so stubborn and won't even admit it even if it is the ruin of us.

Religion says compete to see who can quote the most scriptures.

Relationship declares, "Thy word have I hid in my heart that I might not sin against thee."

Religion teaches one to act so that men may praise you,
Relationship encourages you to please and live for God
and he will reward you.
Lord, please grant me the boldness and courage to fight
against the many demons that fight against me.

I wonder how foolish we must look when we assume that
we are worthy to stand in his wonderful presence.
Some are even so foolish to believe that because they fast
and pray or even dress a certain way, they are worthy.

It's by grace and grace alone that I am able to stand before
him.
Grace that I don't deserve, but have sense to know that it
is mine to have at any time.
Somewhere along the way, we forgot what our purpose is.
The very reason we were molded from clay.
I pray for the day when we all know our purpose and fulfill
it.
Let God's will be done.

I Will Always Remember
(To the memory of my wonderful cousin and friend Cedrick Adams)

I will always remember February 6, 2003.
My cousin passed away that day.
He was not only my cousin, but he was my brother.
Cedrick, I'm not even going to lie.
It took me several months to write this poem.
Because every time I sat down to write, I began to cry.
I cry often when I think of you.
In fact, I'm crying this very moment.
I don't know if I'll ever stop crying.

I thought it was over.
I thought I was ok,
But I'm not.
I lied to everyone at the funeral telling them that I was ok.
It seems that this pain will never go away.
I don't know if I'll ever get over your death.
I still expect to see you whenever I visit the Southside.

I miss you!
I have not only lost a cousin, but a brother and a friend.
I don't even fully understand the concept of God's plan
    for you.
Lord, I said that I wouldn't question you, but this day I
    need an answer.
I need to know why my cousin died.
If you don't give me an answer I ask that you do just one
    thing,
Please embrace our families like never before.

Lord, we need you——I need you
Our aching hearts can't wait another day.

My face is stained with permanent tears.
I not only cry because I miss you,
But I cry for my aunt and uncle who have lost a son.
My cousins who have lost a brother, father, husband and
    friend.
There I go crying again.
I have sat down at least 1000 times to write this poem.
Cedrick, everyone misses you.

Big Girls Have Crushes Too

I love me some Ginuiwine!
He is so fine!
One day I dream of making him mine.

Every time he sings I think he's sing to me.
But that can't be.
Because he didn't marry me,

But Sole,
And I'm happy to say,
I wish the best for them this day.

But at the same time,
I feel she took what was mine.

I'm not going to lie,
But when I heard he got married, I wanted to die.
Then I realized,

This was crazy, because I don't even know the man.
But feel me if you can.

Don't be surprised if one day,
You hear him say,
Sorry Sole,
But I love Paula J.

But for now I guess I will have to stand in line,
With the other 500,000 women who think he's so fine.

Still Missing You

I thought about you the other day.
Come back to me.
I wish you would,
I wish you could,
Come back to me.
I miss you desperately.
It's been too long.
I feel so cheated.
I didn't have enough time to love you,
But in actuality I did.
I just didn't tell you as often as I should have.
We are to use the time we have wisely.
I feel I didn't, but I'm telling you now.
I love you.
I just hope you can hear me.

Grandma, it's been 5 years and I still miss you.
Sometimes, I still cry at night.
I know I have to be strong, but I miss you.
I don't want to even go through this pain again.
The pain of losing someone so dear to me.

So I'll tell you what I asked the Lord today.
Lord, please don't allow dad and mom to go away from
    me.
Please don't take my greatest gift from me.
The gift of having both my dad and mom, here with me.
For if you do, you might as well take me,
Because I will eventually go insane.

I don't even want to see the day when I have to watch
them expire and slowly disappear.
I watched grandma die this way and I can't afford to go
through that again.

Death I hate you!

Someone told me that death has to eat too, but please, not
my parents.
There will be nothing left for me to live for.
All the love I have to give will simply fade away.
I have nothing more to say.

Visions Of Love

Before I even knew you, I saw you in a dream one day.
This is why when I saw you, I was immediately impressed.
When I think of you I'm reminded of paradise,
A wonderful place I would love to be.
You're always good to me.
You make me feel so beautiful and sexy whenever I'm with
you.
Every moment away from you keeps me wanting you.
We have something no one can take.
You've won my heart and I love you.
I hope you can feel what I feel.
Do you want me?
Because I gotta have you.
I need you next to me.
If I must die, I want to die loving you.
I love loving you and it pleases me to please you.
The smile on my face says it all.
I can't take my eyes off of you because I'm in love again.
I thought it would be hard to start over, but you have
made it easy.
God put you here—
Just for me.
I don't know if you will be a blessing or a lesson,
But I do know that I love you.
So please don't deny me your love.
Just a tinge of your love will suffice.
Baby, you know Paula loves you.

Marry Me

This comes straight from the heart,
I can't marry you.
Because I need to be 100% sure before I stand before God
And hundreds of people professing my love to you,
'Til death do us part?
What do I say?
I do?
I don't?
I think?
I don't feel the same way that you do.
How could you be in love with me when I haven't
    returned the favor?
I know you think you love me,
But I don't love you.
I can't go down this road again.
Please know that you will always have a place in my heart.
I can't put myself through this,
And neither can you.

I'm sorry that you are hurting.
I didn't mean to hurt you,
But I must move on.

You're hurting now,
But one day you will look back and thank me for not
    ruining both of our young lives.

Paradisiacal Xperience

It was a lovely evening in September.
A night I will eternally remember.

I was feeling sexy and even naughty.
Anticipating how he was going to ravish my body.

He assumed my favorite position while taking over as my
    one and only lover.
Ripping off the bed sheets and cover.

And as his tongue and lips,
Gently massaged mine below the hips.

I did not want him to stop,
But at the same time, I needed him on top.

Or positioned on my right,
Or me riding all night.

Because I love to ride—horses and bikes.
How he makes my body quiver, I likes.

He had my body pleasantly aching.
Because his lovemaking techniques are so amazing.

I'm screaming Pape,
Why you so good to me?

My body gripped his like a glove.
Because I had been yearning for this kind of love.

As our bodies intertwined,
So were our minds.

I opened wide and took it all night long.
If an Xperience like this isn't right, I'd rather be wrong.

He's coming as I'm coming because we are so in sync.
We come simultaneously because our love is unique.

The kisses continue to come, as does he.
I love it when he explodes inside of me.

He embraces and coddles me,
Loving me endlessly.

For my eyes have seen heaven.
That night we made love 70 times seven.

Heaven has opened its doors and showered on me, indeed.
In fact, I wish heaven would grant me more of these.

This was the most sensual and passionate Xperience ever.
A steamy and pleasant love scene that will play in my
    mind forever.

Message To The Family

Please cremate me.

I don't want anyone staring at my cold, lifeless body.

This is my request.

Lord, I don't ask much,

But if death comes my way,

Please don't allow them to hold a long and drawn out funeral service for me.

I don't want some preacher who didn't even take the time to know me, giving the eulogy.

I don't want someone telling the people the type of life I lived,

Because no one knows but you and I.

It's just that simple.

If they want to do something, please tell them to honor my wish.

Bad, And Oh So Fine

You're bad girl!
You're world is about to exceed you and you must be
    prepared.
You're the bomb and you know it.
You're about to explode!
This is your time and no one can stop it, not even you.
You have stepped out of your boundaries.
And the boxes everyone tried to place you in.
All who step to you must step to you correctly or not at all.
You're bad at everything you do, giving it your all.
You're bad and it doesn't matter who doesn't like it.
You have accomplished things in a couple of years that
    some wait a lifetime to accomplish.
You don't broadcast every single thing you do, how much
    you're worth, or who you're with.
But all who see you know that you are bad and oh so fine!
You go on with your bad self.

Gated Community

I live in a gated community.
Reclusive of this world,
And away from my family,
And the violence.
I feel very safe in this community, but ask me if I'm free.
I'm not free at all.
I'm told when to go to bed and when to get up.
I have several cooks.
They cook me 3 meals a day.
I even got cable.
I'm away from all the problems I used to experience
 because I live in a gated community.

At Times I'm Hated

I never imagined that I would be hated for my looks,
Or the color of my skin among my own race.
I've never imagined walking down the street and receiving
    ugly stares from other females.
Because of my looks or the texture or length of my hair.
Or the shade of my skin.
Some even hate me for what I'm wearing or what I own.
Or maybe it's the large amounts in my back account.
Don't hate on me because I'm a sista that's paid!
I never imagined my sista's being jealous of me.
I knew there was a possibility of me being hated for the
    color of my skin,
By other races, but not my own.
I would say stop hating, but keep hating because it only
    gives me fuel and something to write about.

I realized why I am hated.
You hate me because I know who I am.
You hate me because you hate yourself.
It's true that hatred only destroys the one who hates.
You hate me because I love myself.
You hate me because I know my purpose.
And you have none.
You hate me because you can't relate to me.
You hate and that's fine because you don't have to love me
    because I am in love with myself.
And nothing you say or do can change that.
You don't even have to acknowledge my existence.
But when it's all over, I guarantee you will respect me.

No Matter What

She shared the fact that she had been hurt before.
He hurt her something terrible.
I wouldn't wish these pains of love on my worst enemy.
This is why she's with women now.
I've been hurt before too, but I still love men.
Because I realize that not all men are the same even
    though it may seem like it.
I tried desperately to explain this to her.
She refused, proclaiming that she doesn't need a man.
I do.
Besides who's going to hold me when I'm feeling lonely.
She offers.
I tell her that I don't swing that way.
Because no matter how badly a man treats me,
I can't just give up on men like that.

Tribute To My Many Heroes And Mentors

I remember how long it took to get this far.
I have come a long way.
You've helped me get where I am today.
You helped me accomplish so many things.
And I honor you today and forever.
Thank you for motivating and encouraging me.
I want to thank you for being such bold and courageous individuals,
Paving the way for my strength.
I am glad to know you exist.
Thank you for investing your life in mine.

Senility

You are fading away from me so fast.
Your love is leaving me.
You are slipping my mind so quickly.
I saw it right, but I read it wrong.
These visions of love can be tricky at times.
I saw visions of you and I together eternally.
But now you have slipped away from my mind and me.

Better Man

Now you want to be a better man.

Why you couldn't do it while we were together, I don't
know.

After I've found somebody else who can do the things you
wouldn't do.

You should've treated me right when you had the chance,

But now I'm being loved like I've never been loved.

You act like you love me since I have someone else.

It's funny how the tables have turned on you.

At times, you would make me feel as though I had
committed a crime, when all I requested was some of
your time.

Now you want my time.

Wanting to know who I'm with

And where I'm going.

It's really none of your business.

You just continue to focus on trying to be a better
man—for some other female because I've found my
better man.

Not Hood Enough

I'm not hood enough for you?
Is that what you just said?
Truth be told, you're not good enough for me.
I can't help it because I wasn't raised in the ghetto.
Please excuse me if I don't speak Ebonics.
You do know that not all blacks speak this language.
And not all blacks live in the ghetto.
You are entitled to your opinions and preferences,
But how ignorant you sound when you tell me that I'm
  not hood enough for you.

June 11, 2001

Of all days, he was executed on my day.

Pronounced dead at 7:14 a.m.

I didn't want to watch the execution, but I did.

I remember the sad feelings that had taken over what was supposed to be a happy occasion.

He sat there strapped to the chair several years later after his insidious crime,

Quoting lines from one of my favorite poems as potassium chloride flowed through his entire body.

I knew he should have paid for what he had admitted to several years ago.

The City continues to mourn the 168 lives that were lost as he is laid to rest.

But this was my day.

My birthday.

I Care

If I never tell you now much I care.
Please let this assure you that I do.
If I never tell you that I love you, please know that I do.
If I get too busy and don't take time to say thank you.
Please read these few lines and know that every word is
    true.
If I get too busy to spend a little time, please understand
    that I will never be too busy for those I love.

Evoke My Mind

I know that I'm fine.

This is why I only eat and drink products by Very Fine,
   Inc.

But boyfriend, I need for you to stimulate my mind.

Make love to it.

I need you in my mind.

If "you're so fine" are the only words that can flow from
   your lips,

You are not worth my time.

I need you to stimulate my mind almost all the time.

If you are only in love with my outer beauty, please leave
   now because your feelings are about to get hurt.

Because I am not impressed with the many lines I hear
   everyday.

Labels

How can you want to be so politically correct and add the
    word American to my African label,
But not want to give me the same rights as an American?
America, are you really so great?
You go around with your self-righteous teachings,
    preaching to mankind.
And helping others outside your borders, while the
    homeless and hungry walk your streets daily.
Your neighbor of African decent hungers for your love
    and support.
We are all the same, so why the labels?
I thought I was black,
But I am the Rican in American.
The Africa in African.
I am the America in American.
The Rican in African.
I consider myself Caucasian.
But I am really the Asian in Caucasian.
They said I had to alter my behavior and features to fit in
    with the majority.
It seems as if someone else chose my race.

My People

I love my people!
I love the many different color shades that we come in.
From the darkest to the lightest,
How beautiful are my people.
They have this greatness about them.
A very powerful people.
I love the presence of my people.
Contrary to some thinking less of us,
We are powerful and great.
I LOVE MY PEOPLE!

Locks

I cried for several days because you were laid to rest on
    Saturday, December 6, 2003.
And when it's cold outside,
I still sometimes find myself feeling to see if you are still
    there.
When I feel that breeze, I know you are gone for real.
Years with you makes it painful to part from you.
I know that you will come back one day.
Toss those huge curlers and flat irons right out the
    window.
Don't have enough hair for those styles anymore.
No more tangled shampooed hair.
My flowing locks are gone as of today.

Boyfriend Turned Stalker

Somebody's watching me,
Walking around in disguise.
Eyes of hurt and pain,
Hair disheveled,
Mind insane.
Numbers being changed frequently.
Undisclosed location.
Keeping secrets from family and friends.
Re-occurring nightmares of stalking till I give in have me
living in fear.

At one time, thinking it was cute that you would pop up
unannounced,
But realizing that this was a sign of your distrust hoping
to catch me in an act or a compromising position.
Constantly accusing me of cheating almost all the time.
Even pushing me to it.
But realizing this was your own guilt you tried to hide.
You didn't trust yourself, so how could you trust me.
Even thinking your jealousy was a little cute at one time,
But now realizing that bumping into you everywhere was
not just a coincidence,
But that you were actually keeping tabs on me.
When did you have time to live your life because you were
too busy living mine?
109 messages on my voicemail.
The signs were there, but girlfriend ignored them.

Easily Led

She was so easily led,
To the bed.

Something's missing in her heart.
Been searching for Daddy's love from the start.

Beautiful and not knowing it.
Letting many hit it and hit it.

So easy her legs,
She is willing to spread.

Not careful with whom she shares her feelings, heart and
body with; she allows all to enter her insides.
Soon realizing that the thickness in between their thighs
can sometime tell lies.

She loves the way that lengthy thing rises in between her
undeveloped thighs.
Manifesting her daily highs.

While wondering why a different one makes its way,
Through, almost everyday.

Often exuding milky-white discharges, signs of an STD.
Clouding her vision and sometimes memory.

The fear of conception and diseases have entered the back
of her mind.
Realizing none of them used protection each time.

What were they thinking, or not?
Was it the alcohol or the pot?

Maybe a combination of the both.
This is how it started and on the pressures of life, she
began to choke.

The mere fact that she believed every word,
She heard,

Tells me she didn't understand they were only lies,
To get in between her thighs.

Don't Call Me Nigger!
(For Irene)

It's the 21st Century and someone called me nigger.

What does this say?

What does this mean?

We haven't come as far as we've claimed, it would seem.

I am not a nigger,

But if I continue to be insulted,

I might be justified in showing you one.

We don't sit back anymore.

This is a new day and a new generation.

So don't call me nigger.

The word in its entirety has been deleted from my
vocabulary.

Although, some say the meaning may vary.

It still means the same to me.

So don't call me nigger.

What did I do to deserve such treatment?

To be treated so badly.

If my existence is disturbing you, then leave.

If my existence is killing you, then die.

Because like the tree planted by the rivers of waters, I shall
not be moved.

I'm not the one that has a problem with my skin color.

In fact, I love my beautiful black skin.

If the mere fact of me being born here causes you great
pain, I suggest you leave this country.

Because I was told that I was free here.

But before I let you go, I've got one more question.

Why is it that when some of us walk down the street you lock your car doors or clutch your purses or even speed up almost running away from us?

Shouldn't I be afraid of you because the majority of serial killers look like you?

Untitled 2

I need to apologize,
To all those guys,
To whom I told so many lies.
I'm sorry.
I need to apologize.
I'm sorry for saying Lil' Man was yours when I knew there
was a possibility he wasn't.
I'm sorry for bringing you on those talk shows and
humiliating not only myself, but also you and my
child.
I need very much to apologize,
For all those lies.
I knew you weren't my baby's daddy, but I swore before
millions that I was 110% sure.
Even after all you've done for me.
You were so good to me and I didn't want to lose you, so
I lied.
I knew you weren't the only one I was sleeping with when
Lil' Man was conceived.
So I need to apologize.

My Favorite Girl

As adorable as you want to be.
I love you.
I love to kiss you.
I love when you call me Ti Ti.
I love when you jump up to hug me and never let go.
You make me love you as my own.
You have me considering creating little ones like yourself.
I love you, Miracle!
You are my favorite girl.

I just love loving you.
I love the way you laugh and make me laugh.
Your soft words and harmless play.
I miss you when you are away from me.
You are my sweet and adorable angel.
A delicate little flower I want to call my own.

How Much?

How much can one man bare?
I really don't want to discuss this issue.
Fear that as soon as the words of questioning leave my lips,
The same tragedy will find its way to my door.
You've lost your father, mother and now your brother all
    in one year.
I don't know how much more you can bare.
But I know that God comforts like no other.

The Parish Has Perished

I see the lust in your eyes,
As you look at that 9-year-old's thighs.

You are a sick pervert with distorted inventions.
Using your collar to disguise your true intentions.

So many have been scarred from your false teachings.
You have not been practicing what you've been preaching.

But you've been practicing and practicing with little boys
    and girls of your parish.
Without a true follower of God, the people indeed perish.

This Is Goodbye

You always seem to hold me back.
So it's time for you to bounce.
I stood by you for 12 long years.
Nothing but hurt and pain.
You abused me in every way possible.
At times making me feel worthless.
Sadly, you are not the only one to blame.
I kept letting you back in each time you apologized or
    sang me out of my panties.
It wasn't love at all that allowed me to subject myself to
    such abuse.
Low self-esteem is something terrible.
I'm tired of you and I can't take it any more.
This is like a sad song, but I must move on.
So baby, this is goodbye.
I cried because a part of me had died.
Sadness was never one of my emotions, the night I left.
Happiness was there because the old me had passed away.
And honestly, I can't cry any more.

No More Love

Let me explain the reason I have to leave.

Love for you isn't here anymore.

I must move on and you should do the same.

Because this once amicable relationship has become very
bitter.

It's not hard to see that I need to be free.

Please, let me breathe.

You have to get closure.

I don't know what more I can say.

You want desperately what you cannot have.

Let it go.

Let it go.

I'm not going to tell you that it's not going to hurt because
it will.

The feelings that I once had for you have dissipated into
the air.

Love doesn't live here any more.

I've learned to listen to my heart and my heart doesn't lie.

I don't love you.

Although, you want me to tell you, I can't tell you that I
do.

I can't lie to you or myself.

I can't live a lie.

I won't live a lie.

My heart won't let me.

I can't love you the way you want me to.

I wish you the best in finding someone who can.

Riding The L

On the platform there's a brotha so fine staring at me.
He stands on the platform waiting for his train as I check
out his form.
I think he works in my building so I retreat.
I have something against dating co-workers.

On the train there's this homeless man who begs all night
long.
He once told me that people in real need are too
embarrassed to beg for money or food.
I guess he was trying to warn me of the many people who
prey on some of our kindness.
However true, I'm not moved by sympathy to give.
I give when led to.

A few seats down, many witness the shame and
embarrassment in this woman's eyes.
She's blurting out all types of profanity.
I wonder how it is that she got this way.
Was she born mentally ill?
Or did something tragic in life trigger this mind crippling
disease?
She yells at the top of her lungs as some look and others
just ignore this painful experience.

Directly across from me, I am forced into a conversation
with an ex-con.
He tells me of his daily struggles.
I dread to see him sing this very sad song.

Directly behind me there is a man holding a conversation with himself and Lord knows how many other personalities.

While the homeless man from earlier goes from cart to cart hoping that someone will sympathize with him and help him out to get a meal.

At that moment I am moved to thank God for everything he has done for me without asking Him for a thing.

Secret Life

There's this sanctified girl who pleads with all the worldly
boys to let her rock their world.
All the religious men in the church want to marry her
because she's so pure and untouched.
These men want to touch her in man different ways.

But let me tell you about this sanctified boy who watches
the porn flicks,
And then touches himself.
He's done this so long he doesn't even know how to get
excited from a real woman.

They've both been taught well,
To be great pretenders that is.

They are only "saved" on Sundays or in front of you.
Why do you suppose that they are so preoccupied with
trying to please you and the church, when God is the
only one who can judge them correctly?

Could it be the fact that you pound in their heads that
God hates sin?
Because they are so busy with pleasing you, they don't
read the word for themselves,
And you failed to let them know that God's mercies are
renewed daily.

Tribute To Musiq

I love Musiq.
A good song to write to,
Beats to release my inner self,
And lyrics to relax my mind.
Because you sing, I write.
I have found my passion,
My love and this is the reason I write.
Not only through words, but Musiq, sometimes my
  inspiration.
Without Musiq, what would life be like?
I'm thankful to have you in my life.
As you live on in my life, I continue to write.
Your talents shared through tunes.
My gift through words and thoughts.
As the amazing lyrics flow from your lips.
So does the words from my heart.
You hold the mike,
I the pen,
Expressing words of love.
I continue to be me with out interruptions.
Because you sing, I write.

Thug Song

I'm a thug!
See my pants hang low.
I call women b's and ho's.

But I ain't really no thug.
Tupac,
My thug and a true gangsta, not a wangsta.
Not one to pretend in the streets.
He truly had a rough life.
I can only pretend that I got it tough.

But on the real, I don't want it so bad that I'm willing to
    die for it.
Tupac was and he did.
This is what makes him a true thug.
Me, I'm just a kid from the suburbs perpetrating.

My Favorite Guy

You're not my only, but you're my favorite.

The others don't share what we share.

When we touch there's so much passion that flows
  through our bodies.

Emotions that I normally can control,

But when I'm with you I can't contain myself.

So I indulge.

You're incredible, baby.

You're my favorite guy.

I can't quite place my finger on it, but wow!

We vibe like nothing I've ever seen before.

There's a connection that I've never shared with another
  man.

You're not my only, but it feels like it.

Loving This Man

Trust me if you can,
When I say I truly love this man.

I love the way he's got my back.
In his support, he's not so lax.

Lackadaisical that is.
I handle mine and he definitely handles his.

He's got my back, as well as my front.
A man like this, a woman would be a fool not to want.

But you see, this one is all mine.
He's not one to whine,
Simply, about how I spend my time.

Plus he gives me my space.
Doesn't smother me and be all up in my face.

Ain't no faking.
He's has me palpitating,
About his lovemaking.

I just love the way he makes me feel.
It's not a "hit it and quit it" thing, this love is real.

If ever I get out of line,
He has this tool he whips out from time to time.

It's loooong and wiiide.
And sometimes he tries to hide.

That checkbook, but I always seem to find that thing.
And when I do, boy do I sing.

A song of happiness,
Because I feel so blessed,

To have him in my life.
I'm thankful he made me his wife.

Why is it that I love this man so?
The love I have for him is more than anyone will ever
    know.

41 Shots

Pop, pop, pop, pop, pop!
41 shots.
41 shots.
Pop, pop, pop, pop, pop!
That's all he got.
No explanation.
No justice.

The sound keeps ringing in the back of my head.
The shots that I heard the other day were not from some
    gang, but from the guns of New York's finest.

Bullet wounds were even found in the heels of his feet.
An indication that he was already down and gone,
But each time the trigger was pulled, and a bullet released,
    he died over and over again.

He surrendered without knowing because he was already
    dead.

A 23 year old murdered for no reason.
His bullet-punctured body has many wondering why.

Who would have thought that reaching for your wallet to
    identify yourself would cause you to be shot at 41
    times.

He received 19 shots of the 41 one given and meant to kill
    him.

Mr. & Mrs. Diallo, I have no explanation for you, but my
heart goes out to you and all who have been the victims
of injustice.

In fact, no one can really explain why he had to go out this
way.

Can anyone give me a reason as to why this tragedy
occurred?
Or is it all just a blur because no one is too disturbed?

Ghetto, Not So Fabulous

There is nothing great about the ghetto.
You can add the word fabulous to the end of it,
But there is still nothing wonderful about it.
It's okay to be proud of where you come from,
And don't forget how you got where you are today,
But don't confuse the two.
There is nothing great about a poverty stricken
community.
I've never heard of anything more absurd.
Especially coming from someone who in fact have never
stepped foot inside the ghetto.
What's so lavishing about impoverished men and women
who can't provide for their children?
This is not the way life was intended to be.
It doesn't have to be this way at all.
Don't let them fool you.
Some of them wouldn't even think about stepping foot in
your town.
Stop trying to be like them because while you're trying to
get yours, they already have theirs.
I don't care how many songs you hear about how
wonderful the ghetto is.
It's not so, just ask little Tina whose home doesn't have
heat during Chicago's cold winters.
Or 5 year-old Alex, who hasn't eaten in several days.
Maybe you should asked the seven children who have
been left home alone,
Living in squander conditions fighting off rats and
roaches.

Get hip to the obvious.
Don't make light of a very serious situation.

Get Out Of My Face!

I'm not impressed,
More or less.
I don't even care about how much money you have,
Or the Benz you drive.
In fact, my Bentley along with my driver is parked
    outside.
I'm not impressed with your status.
Or the material things you own.
I'm sorry, but you will have to approach me better than
    that.
You can't move me with such nonsense.
First, you're concerned if I'm high-maintenance or not.
I haven't even answered your first question yet.
Stealing lyrics like, "Excuse me, Miss, can I take you out
    tonight?" and "I can read your mind, baby."
Well, if you could read my mind,
You wouldn't still be standing in my face.
Secondly, you assumed that I was some kind of gold
    digger because I like to look nice.
Even if you wanted to afford me, you couldn't.
Don't ever step to me that way again.
I have my own loot and I don't need yours.
Plus anything I want, I get for myself.
You look shocked.
What's wrong with that?
I'm not saying I'm anti-men, but I'm anti-jerks.
So get out of my face!

You'll Never Hurt

I know you've been hurt before, but I need you to trust
   me.
We've all been hurt at some point before.
I once was afraid to love, just like you because every time
   I opened my heart, it was broken.
But I now know that I can't hide from true love.
And baby I love you.
I need you to let me love you like no other has loved you.
I want to help you love again
Let me love you.
Don't be afraid, but trust me.
I won't hurt you like she did.
As long as you're with me, you'll never hurt.

No Love

I promise you that I'm not a ho.
It's just that I don't know,

Who my father is,
Plus, my sister and I were raped as kids.

I know it's only an excuse,
But it is one of the main reasons for my drug use.

And the reason I sleep around.
Letting all these men lay me down.

Many men of different races.
I'm searching for daddy's love in all the wrong places.

I'm not at all intelligent, but I'm pretty and sexy.
My eyes and young body scream, "Look at me!"

If they don't, I'll make them want me, by giving them
    something they can feel.
Even if I know their love isn't at all real.

I'll just keep telling myself the lie that unreal love is better
    than no love at all.
Sex without love first, has become my downfall.

Keep It Real

She said she dated outside her race one time and one time
only.

Dated a white man and it didn't work out.

He was occupied with "trying to be black" instead of
being himself.

This was a very busy and confusing relationship because
while he was "trying to be black", she was "trying to be
white".

He wasn't "white enough" for her and she wasn't "black
enough" for him.

She explained that if she wanted a "real thug", she would
have taken a ride through the hood.

He also shared that if he wanted a "conservative chick", he
would have taken a stroll through a white-collar
suburb.

Heavenly Body

The other day, someone asked me for the directions to my home.

He said, "Can you tell me how to get to Pleasant Street?"

I responded, "Listen carefully, this is how you get there."

First know that you will enjoy this safari as I take you there.

It's necessary that you must first stimulate my mind.

As you do this, you can bless my lips with sensual kisses.

Then make your way down this very long and narrow main street.

Which can be a teaser and a pleaser.

I must warn you not to be alarmed by the two humps in the street.

In fact please take a few moments to observe and enjoy the alluring mountains & hills.

Many are often distracted because they are so soft and beautiful.

After all, who would expect two bumps in the road to be so smooth?

Next you will come to a hole in the street as you make your way down a few blocks.

Some quickly swerve around this hole in a hurry to get to my home.

But this is a very significant spot.

So please take the time to sip and taste the wine that was so delicately placed there.

Because my home is not very far from this area.

In fact, you are almost at Pleasant Street.

After you have done all of this and as I come—

I mean as you come to my home, you may now enter.
But you must remember that I don't let everyone in my
home.

Too Soon

If we had something,
You ruined it for the both of us because you gave it up too
easily and quickly.
Some say I have the mentality of a male.
Others call me a dog because I will do a hit and run in a
minute.
Especially when you give it up so easily.
I have no respect for you because you have no respect for
yourself.
The little respect that I did have quickly evaporated, the
night you gave it up so easily.
You bragged about how the girls you knew for a day ended
up in your bed the next night.
You refer to them as ho's now.
Yet I only knew you for 2 hours and you gave me some.
What does that make you?

Kill The Voices

The depressing feelings and the hurt that I tried to
   suppress have resurfaced once again.
So have the suicidal thoughts.
They tell me to kill the voices that keep taunting me.
The voices are telling me to kill myself.
Although, I'm afraid to go through with it, I want to.
But the fear of a third unsuccessful attempt is consuming
   me.
The pain of having to live again, when I don't even want
   to.
I can't hold on anymore.
I am slowly slipping through the cracks.
But death or life is my decision as I am reminded of my 3
   beautiful children sleeping in the next room.
They can't be without their mother too.
Daddy has already taken that route.

If Ever...

If ever I need someone, this is what I need:
A man who has no problem with allowing me to be me.
Allowing me to be free.
He must understand that he can't smother me.
This will only hide the true me,
Leading me away from him because I can't afford to
    suffocate my dreams.
He must be so confident in himself that when others try
    to take what's his, he doesn't sweat it because he knows
    he has my heart and I'm not going anywhere.
He must be so incredible to the point that I can't bare to
    leave him.

I'm Not Trying To Be Rude, But...

Is that all you want to do?
Is that all you want to do?
Is it?
You might as well want to.
Everyone else just wants to hit this.
I am so sick of everyone trying to hit this.
Both men and women,
Old and young.
You didn't answer me, is that all you want to do?

Bold, but embarrassed at this point, she responds, "I'm
    not trying to be rude, but yes."

No Explanation

I never thought that it would be me.

For I have committed adultery.

I have cheated on the man of my dreams.

Me, the most ethical person alive.

I feel so dirty.

I disgust myself.

Someone asked me if women cheat.

Take it from me, they do.

Men are often accused of cheating, but this time a female
is the culprit.

I have no excuse or explanation for this infidelity.

It seems that I have destroyed this man and this marriage.

I had a moment of weakness and I'm sorry.

You want and need an explanation.

I have none.

As Many Times Is Her Pain

You see this beautiful face and gorgeous body.
If she looks like a model in your eyes, you are in for a big
  surprise.
She has so many scars she successfully hides.
She looks very good on the outside, but her beauty is sure
  to tell lies.

You say you want to "tap that" and do all kinds of things
  to her.
But this woman hides a very dark and deep secret.
You don't see the scars that live beneath the beauty of this
  being.
All you see is that gorgeous face and bodacious body.
She regrets trusting him to the point where she let him hit
  it raw.
He pleaded and begged her to let him feel her without any
  interference.
"It just doesn't feel the same", He begged.
She concurred.
And now she's dying.
Many only see her outward beauty.
They can't see the pain that makes a grown woman cry.
He hit it raw over and over again.
As many times is her pain.

How could she let him do this?
Because she never imagined that such an ugly disease
  could affect a beautiful woman.
I guess she was willing to sell her soul because it was in.
Not realizing that her life is too precious.

I Can't

The word can't is not in my vocabulary,
But there is something that I can't do.
I can't do time.
If I ever get convicted and sentenced to prison, I'll die.
I 'd rather die.
In fact, you might as well kill me immediately because I
    can't do time.
I can't exist in prison.
My body was not built for prison.

Years Ago

Years ago, he used to love me.

Where did all that love go?

Was it transferred to another woman?

I wonder if it will ever make its way back to me.

I tried to hold on to what was left of it, but when I looked
    in his eyes,

I knew that love no longer lived here.

Already knowing the answer, I foolishly questioned him
    why.

He doesn't love me anymore like he used to.

I see this, but I still don't believe it.

I still love him.

I don't think I can love anyone else the way that I have
    loved this man.

He killed me with his kisses each time his lips met mine.

It hurts to start again.

Because I have loved this man so deeply and so long.

I can love no other.

I am just so tired of being tired.

I was there for him during his times of pain and suffering.

I held him down when things got rough.

What he had was good.

Remember, baby, I will always love you.

S.A.D

"You ain't nothing."

"And you ain't never gonna be."

"You're SAD."

"A stupid a*% dummy."

His father used to tell him this all the time.

These words ring in the back of his mind relentlessly.

He doesn't even swear since he had his own little boy.

This is why he can't bring himself to say the second word.

Not only that, but it's very painful to remember.

These three little words continue to haunt this grown man
who now has a family of his own.

He is so determined not to be like his father or sperm
donor as he calls him.

In fact, I pray that he doesn't treat our child the way his
father treated him.

So Close

You were so close to winning my heart completely.

But then you had to go and mess up.

Actually, I'm glad it happened before I committed myself
  solely to you.

You hurt me, but it helped me to love myself.

You were so close

You almost had me.

But we all know that almost doesn't count.

Can't Hurt Again

I have to protect my heart.
This is why my feelings are hidden deep within.
I can't get hurt anymore.

Once I knew hurt and I don't want that again.
Almost causing me to lose my life.
I once fell very hard for a man.
I promised myself that I would never do that again.
I hope this doesn't affect me finding my true love.
Because I'm definitely not looking for him, at least not
    right now.
I refuse to go through the hurt and pain once more.
Lord knows I've been through it before.
Once lying at death's door.
All I could think about was this man.
I just wanted to be with him.
I loved him so hard.
And hard I fell.
It was something terrible.
He obviously didn't feel the same.
He couldn't even imagine my pain.
Does anyone care?
I don't know if I will ever be able to love again.
The scars are already there.
I can't forget because the pain has set in.
I became depressed and I didn't want to live anymore.
My demise was not at all exaggerated.
I waited at death's doorstep as my life became replete with
    feelings of loneliness.
I can't go through that again.

I won't.

I'm not sure if I will be able to recover a second time
around.

For The Last Time

My father killed my mother.
And now my father is dead.
I lost both my parents on the same day.
He beat my mother to death.
Now he's dead.
Daddy hit mommy for the last time today.

Not A Playa

I haven't given up on love, but I know what I want.
And you are not the one.
So you choose to label me as a bitter and scorned woman.
You mistake my independence for not wanting or needing
a man.
I never said that I don't need a man.
You have made another wrong assumption.
Someone once said that assumptions makes an a#% out of
us.
If you knew anything about me, you would know that I
love men.
But just because I don't want you, you choose to label me.
Calling me a playa because I choose not to marry.
What's that all about?
When did taking a moment out to love yourself, become
one of a playa's characteristics?

If You Promise...

If you promise not to make me a bitter woman, I promise
I will love you.

Don't make me regret loving you.

If you promise not to bring up your past hurts, I promise
not to make you pay for what my ex's did.

Don't make me regret giving you my heart.

Don't make me love you completely then you bounce.

Don't make me feel like I've committed a crime when I
request a little bit of your time.

I don't want to brag about how wonderful you are and
then you let me down.

I want to love you, but you must first promise.

Loving Me

It hasn't always been easy loving me.
But the time has come for me to sit and evaluate myself.
Self-love is second to God's love.
He has given me the power to love myself.
If ever I want to love someone else,
I must first love myself.
Loving me is the best thing I could do.
I can't fully love someone else until I know how to love
    myself.
You can't get the best of me, without me giving it.
That starts with me loving me first.
I can't commit to you until I have committed to myself.
I need to be happy with me before I please you.
I love loving me.
Let me reiterate,
I love loving me.
Some people wait a lifetime to find true love.
I have found true love within myself after searching for
    several years.
At this point in my life, I am completely in love with
    myself.
I am dating Paula Denise Johnson and it is wonderful.
I am one of a kind.
Love has changed my life.
I never knew a love so great.
My love.

About the Author

Paula D. Johnson burst onto the poetry scene with the publication of her first book entitled, *Poetry Is More Than Just a Poem*, in 2002. She received an International Poet of Merit Award from the International Society of Poets. Johnson was also one of the nominees to replace Gwendolyn Brooks for the distinguished position of Illinois Poet Laureate. She is a life-long resident of Illinois who makes numerous appearances at local schools and serves the Chicago adult community as a volunteer for Literacy Chicago which is the largest adult literacy organization in Illinois. Also serving in mentoring programs throughout Chicago, such as the Boys & Girls Clubs Mentoring Program, "helping young people successfully make the transition from youth to adulthood." She is currently working on a play and short stories. Johnson earned a B.A. in psychology at Elmhurst College and she is employed at the Illinois Attorney General's Office.

0-595-31402-3